Oxford
International
First
Atlas

Editorial Adviser
Dr Patrick Wiegand

OXFORD
UNIVERSITY PRESS

Great Clarendon Street, Oxford OX2 6DP

Oxford University Press is a department of the University of Oxford.
It furthers the University's objective of excellence in research, scholarship,
and education by publishing worldwide in

Oxford   New York

Auckland Cape Town Dar es Salaam Hong Kong Karachi
Kuala Lumpur Madrid Melbourne Mexico City Nairobi
New Delhi Shanghai Taipei Toronto

With offices in

Argentina Austria Brazil Chile Czech Republic France Greece
Guatemala Hungary Italy Japan Poland Portugal Singapore
South Korea Switzerland Thailand Turkey Ukraine Vietnam

Oxford is a registered trade mark of Oxford University Press
in the UK and in certain other countries

ISBN 978 0 19 848020 4

3 5 7 9 10 8 6 4 2

Printed in Singapore by KHL Printing Co. Pte Ltd.

Paper used in the production of this book is a natural, recyclable product
made from wood grown in sustainable forests. The manufacturing process
conforms to the environmental regulations of the country of origin.

Acknowledgements

The publishers would like to thank Roderick Hunt for his advice on literacy levels.

The publishers and author would like to thank the following:
p2tl: Corbis/Digital Stock/OUP; **p2tr:** Image Source/OUP; **p2cl:** Photodisc/OUP; **p2cr:** Photodisc/OUP; **p2bl:** Digital Vision/OUP; **p2br:** Photodisc/OUP;
p5: Planetary Visions Ltd/Science Photo Library; **p6:** Planetary Visions Ltd/Science Photo Library; **p8tl:** Planetary Visions Ltd/Science Photo Library;
p8br: Planetary Visions Ltd/Science Photo Library; **p9:** OUP; **p10:** PlanetObserver/Science Photo Library; **p11:** PlanetObserver/Science Photo Library;
p13: Richard Cracknell 01/classic/Alamy; **p20:** Obstando Images/Alamy; **p23:** OUP; **p25:** Jochen Tack/ImageBroker/PhotoLibrary; **p26:** Visions of America,
LLC/Alamy; **p27:** Gary Cook/Alamy; **p29:** Dave Watts/Alamy; **p30:** Peter Arnold, Inc./Alamy; **p31:** Steven J. Kazlowski/Alamy; **p32tl:** George
Steinmetz/Science Photo Library; **p32tr:** Josh Landis/National Science Foundation; **p32bl:** Nick Haslam/Alamy; **p32br:** David Nunuk/Science Photo Library

Illustrations by Mark Brierley.

Cover illustrations by Galia Bernstein. Cover globe by Jan Rysavy/iStockphoto.

Contents

Greetings from THE ALPS

Look at pages 22–23.

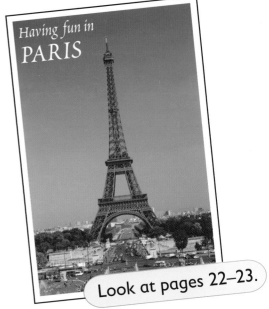

Having fun in PARIS

Look at pages 22–23.

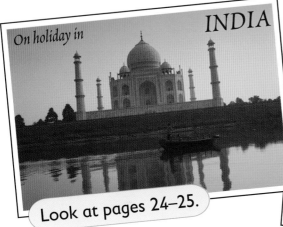

On holiday in INDIA

Look at pages 24–25.

A postcard from NEW YORK

Look at page 26.

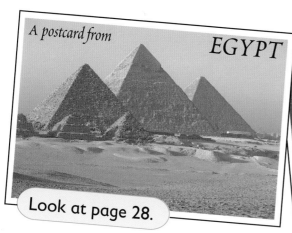

A postcard from EGYPT

Look at page 28.

Greetings from PERU

Look at page 27.

2   Can you find these places in the atlas?

4   This is space.

The Earth is a planet in space.

5

6   The Earth is round, like a ball.

Satellites take pictures of the Earth.

You can see the
whole world.

You can zoom
in close.

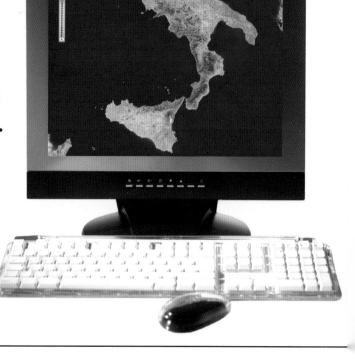

These are satellite pictures on a computer.

The Earth has land and sea.

A globe is a model of the Earth.

The World

This is a picture of the Earth from space.

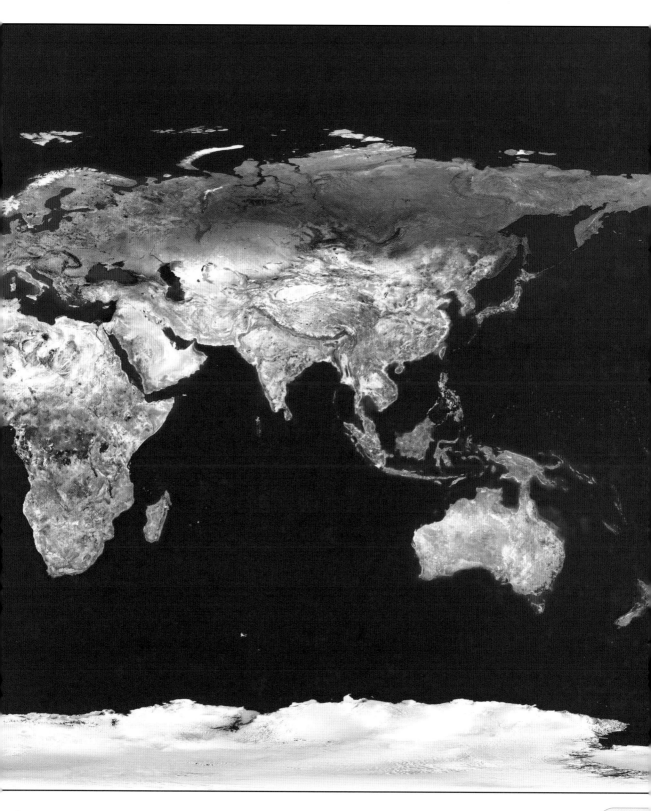

It is laid out flat.

The World

Key
- ∿ river
- ⋀ mountains
- ⋄ desert

Rocky Mountains

River Missisippi

Atlantic Ocean

Sah

Pacific Ocean

River Amazon

Andes

Atlantic Ocean

Southern Ocean

This is a map of the world.

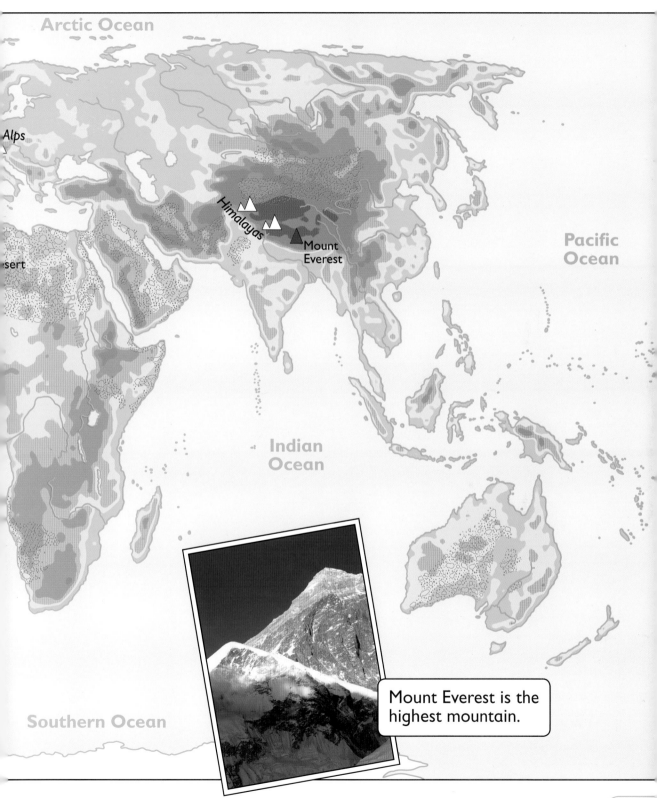

Arctic Ocean

Alps

Himalayas

Mount
Everest

Pacific
Ocean

sert

River Nile

Indian
Ocean

Mount Everest is the
highest mountain.

Southern Ocean

It shows rivers, mountains and deserts.

The World

North America

South America

This is a map of Antarctica.

Antarctica

South Pole

The world has seven continents.

Europe

Asia

Africa

Oceania

Antarctica

Continents are very big areas of land.

The World

North America

Rocky Mountains

River Mississippi

Atlantic Ocean

Pacific Ocean

River Amazon

South America

Atlantic Ocean

Andes

Southern Ocean

Sah

Key

	fox
	squirrel
	camel
	panda
	tiger
	giraffe
	howler monkey
	Andean condor
	polar bear
	kangaroo
	crocodile
	penguin
	whale
	bobcat
	grey wolf

Animals live everywhere on Earth.

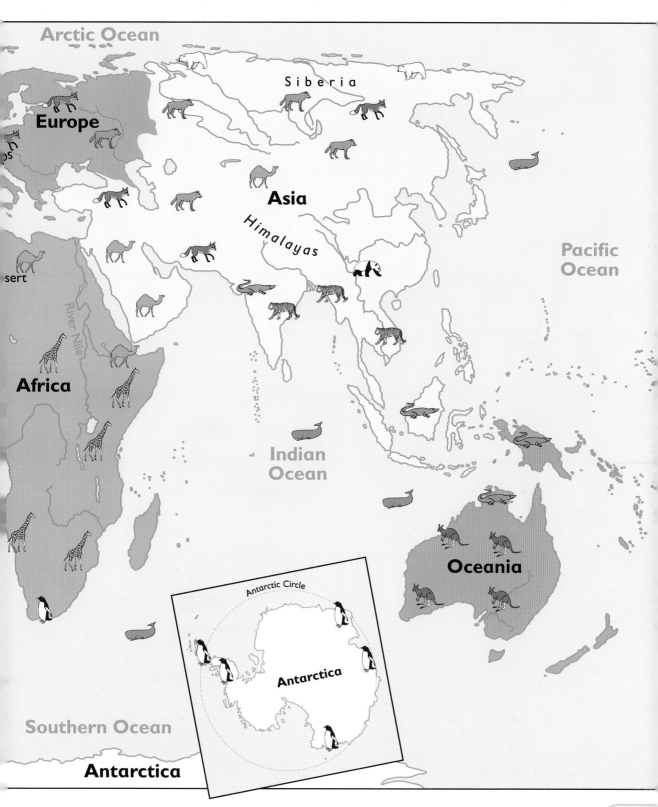

Arctic Ocean

Siberia

Europe

Asia

Himalayas

Pacific Ocean

sert

River Nile

Africa

Indian Ocean

Oceania

Antarctic Circle

Antarctica

Southern Ocean

Antarctica

Each animal needs its own place to live.

The World

Canada

United Kingdom

Fra...

Spai...

United States of America

Morocco

Mexico

Ma...

Colombia

Brazil

Peru

Bolivia

Chile

Argentina

Key

Colours show countries.

The world has many countries.

Russia

Japan

China

Iran

Pakistan

ly

Libya

Egypt

Saudi Arabia

India

Philippines

Chad

Sudan

South Sudan

Ethiopia

Kenya

Tanzania

Angola

Madagascar

Indonesia

Australia

South Africa

New Zealand

Which country are you from?

The World

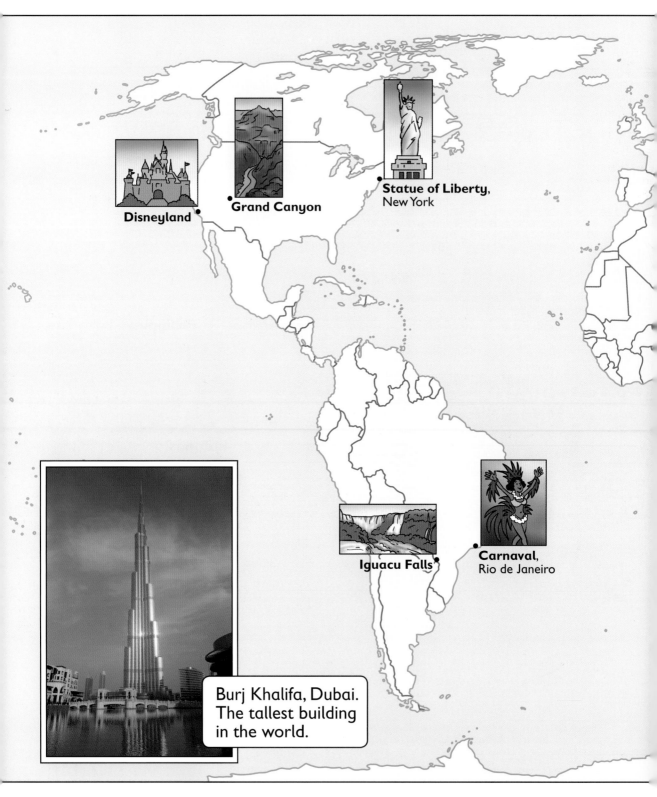

Disneyland

Grand Canyon

Statue of Liberty, New York

Iguacu Falls

Carnaval, Rio de Janeiro

Burj Khalifa, Dubai. The tallest building in the world.

There are many places in the world to visit

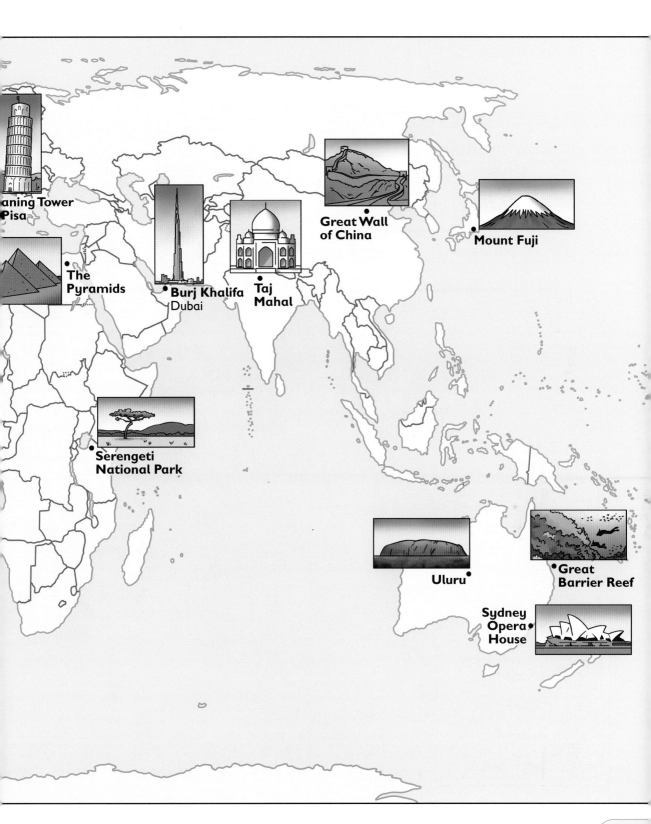

Leaning Tower of Pisa

The Pyramids

Burj Khalifa
Dubai

Taj Mahal

Great Wall of China

Mount Fuji

Serengeti National Park

Uluru

Great Barrier Reef

Sydney Opera House

Where would you like to go?

Europe

Iceland
■Reykjavik

Sweden

Norway

Oslo■

Stockholm

Denmark

■Copenhagen

United
Kingdom

Republic
of Ireland

Dublin■

Amsterdam
■

Berlin ■

Polan

London
■

Netherlands

Germany

■Brussels
Belgium

Prague ■ Czech
Republi

Paris
■

River Danube

Vienn

Bern
Switzerland

Austria

Slovenia

Croo

Alps

Bosnia
Herzego
Saraje

France

Italy

Monten

■Rome

Key

Colours show
countries.

■ capital cities

river

△△ mountains

Madrid
■

Portugal

Spain

Lisbon■

Malto

Europe is a small continent.

Finland

Helsinki

Tallinn
Estonia

Riga
Latvia

Lithuania
Vilnius

Minsk

Belarus

Russia

Moscow

River Volga

arsaw

Kiev

Ukraine

akia

Moldova

ngary

Chisinau

Romania

elgrade

Bucharest

bia

osovo

Bulgaria
Sofia

FYRO
acedonia

ania

Greece

Athens

Ankara

Turkey

Cyprus

Georgia
Tbilisi

Hello   Hola   Buon giorno

God dag   Guten Tag

Bonjour   Yia sas

Dzień dobry   Merhaba

There are many European languages.

Asia

Russia

Moscow

Astana

Kazakhstan

Ulan Bator
Mongolia

Bishkek
Uzbekistan Tashkent
Kyrgyzstan
Armenia Azerbaijan Turkmenistan Dushanbe Tajikistan Gobi Desert Beijing

Ashgabat Kabul China Pyongyo
Syria Afghanistan
Damascus Baghdad Tehran Islamabad
Israel Iraq Amman Iran
Jordan Kuwait Pakistan Himalayas
Saudi Qatar New Nepal Yangtze River
Arabia Delhi Bhutan
Riyadh United Arab Muscat Bangladesh Hanoi
Emirates Dhaka Myanmar Laos
Oman India Vientiane
Yemen Yangon Thailand Manila
Sana Bangkok Cambodia Vietnam Philippines

Sri Lanka Malaysia
Colombo Kuala Lumpur

Jakarta Indonesi

Asia is the largest continent.

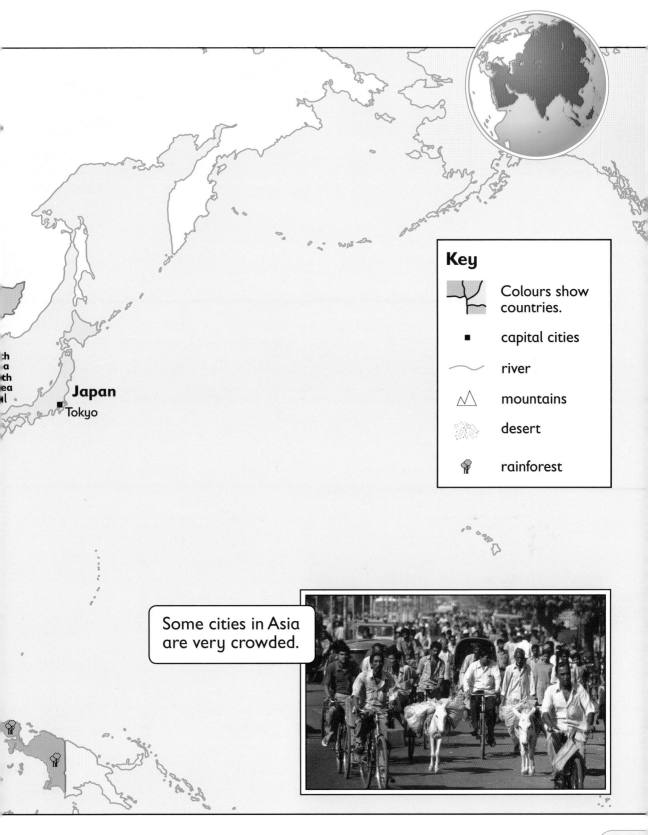

Japan
■ Tokyo

Key

Colours show countries.

■ capital cities

～ river

⋀ mountains

desert

🌳 rainforest

Some cities in Asia
are very crowded.

It also has the most people.

North America

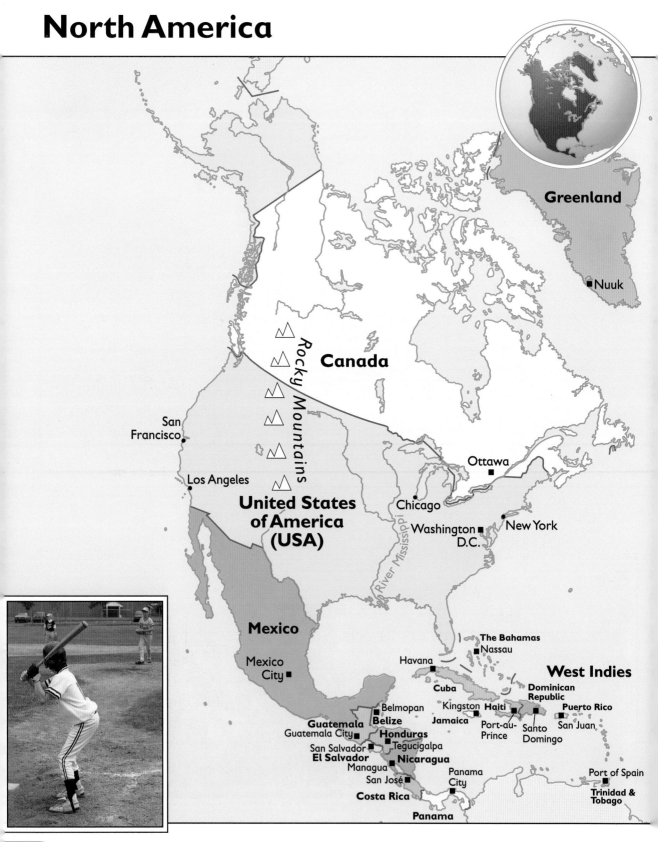

Greenland

Nuuk

Canada

Rocky Mountains

San Francisco

Los Angeles

Ottawa

Chicago

United States of America (USA)

Washington D.C.

New York

River Mississippi

Mexico

Mexico City

Havana

Cuba

The Bahamas
Nassau

West Indies

Dominican Republic

Kingston

Haiti

Puerto Rico

Belmopan

Belize

Jamaica

Port-au-Prince

Santo Domingo

San Juan

Guatemala
Guatemala City

Honduras

Tegucigalpa

San Salvador

El Salvador

Nicaragua

Managua

San José

Panama City

Port of Spain

Costa Rica

Trinidad & Tobago

Panama

The USA is the world's richest country.

South America

Caracas

Venezuela

Georgetown

Paramaribo
Cayenne

Bogota

Colombia

Guyana

Suriname

French Guiana

Quito
Ecuador

River Amazon

B r a z i l

Lima

Peru

A
n
d
e
s

Bolivia

La Paz

Brasilia

Paraguay

Sao Paulo

Asuncion

Rio de Janeiro

A
n
d
e
s

C
h
i
l
e

Argentina

Santiago

Uruguay

Buenos Aires

Montevideo

A
n
d
e
s

Key

Colours show countries.

■   capital cities

•   other cities

～   river

⋀   mountains

🌳   rainforest

It rains a lot in the Amazon rainforest.

There is a big rainforest in Brazil.

Africa

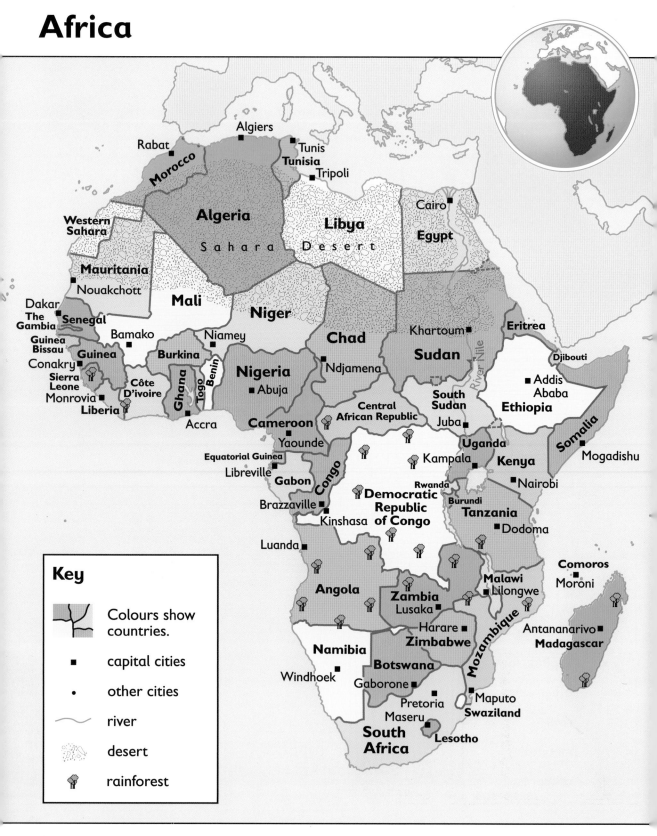

Rabat
Algiers
Tunis
Tunisia
Tripoli
Cairo
Morocco
Algeria
Libya
Egypt
S a h a r a   D e s e r t
Western Sahara
Mauritania
Nouakchott
Mali
Niger
Chad
Khartoum
Eritrea
Dakar
The Gambia
Senegal
Bamako
Niamey
Sudan
Djibouti
Guinea Bissau
Guinea
Burkina
Nigeria
Ndjamena
River Nile
Addis Ababa
Conakry
Sierra Leone
Côte D'ivoire
Ghana
Togo
Benin
Abuja
South Sudan
Ethiopia
Monrovia
Liberia
Accra
Cameroon
Juba
Somalia
Yaounde
Central African Republic
Uganda
Kenya
Mogadishu
Equatorial Guinea
Libreville
Gabon
Congo
Kampala
Nairobi
Rwanda
Democratic Republic of Congo
Burundi
Tanzania
Brazzaville
Kinshasa
Dodoma
Luanda
Comoros
Moroni
Angola
Zambia
Malawi
Lilongwe
Lusaka
Harare
Mozambique
Antananarivo
Madagascar
Zimbabwe
Namibia
Botswana
Windhoek
Gaborone
Maputo
Pretoria
Swaziland
Maseru
South Africa
Lesotho

Key

Colours show countries.

■ capital cities

• other cities

~ river

desert

🌳 rainforest

Africa is the hottest continent.

Oceania

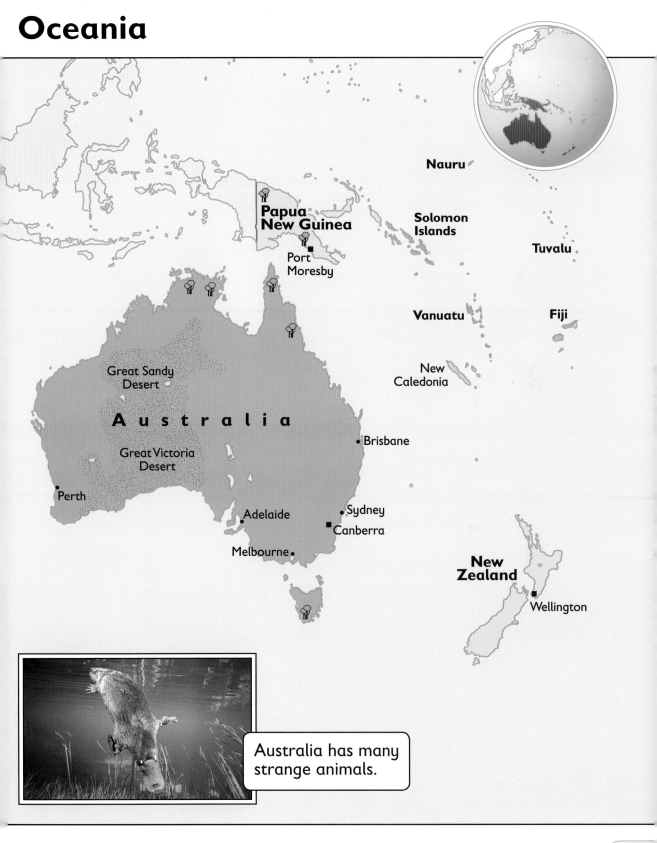

Nauru

Papua New Guinea

Port Moresby

Solomon Islands

Tuvalu

Vanuatu

Fiji

New Caledonia

Great Sandy Desert

A u s t r a l i a

Great Victoria Desert

Perth

•Brisbane

Adelaide

•Sydney
Canberra

Melbourne•

New Zealand

Wellington

Australia has many strange animals.

There are lots of islands in Oceania.

Antarctica

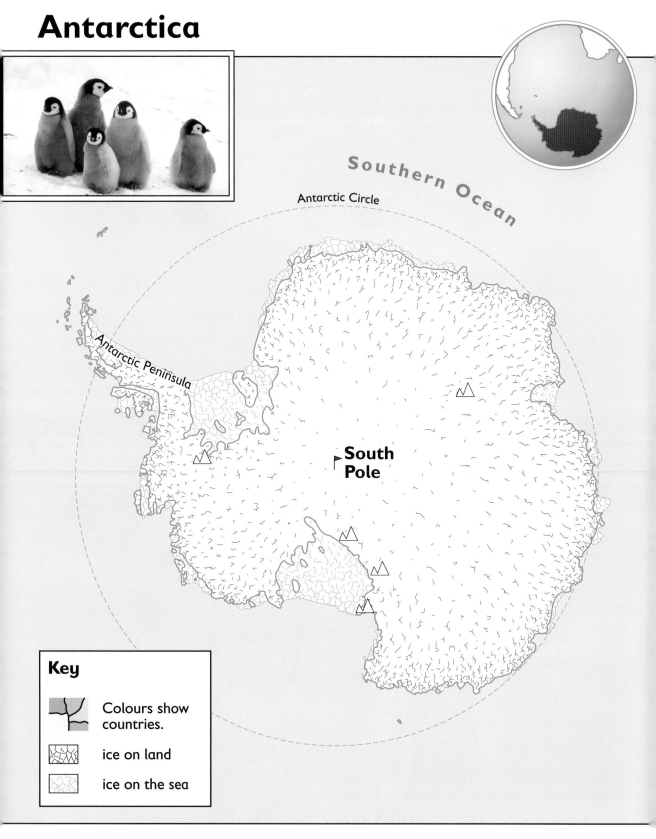

Southern Ocean

Antarctic Circle

Antarctic Peninsula

South Pole

Key

Colours show countries.

ice on land

ice on the sea

Antarctica is land covered in ice.

The Arctic Ocean

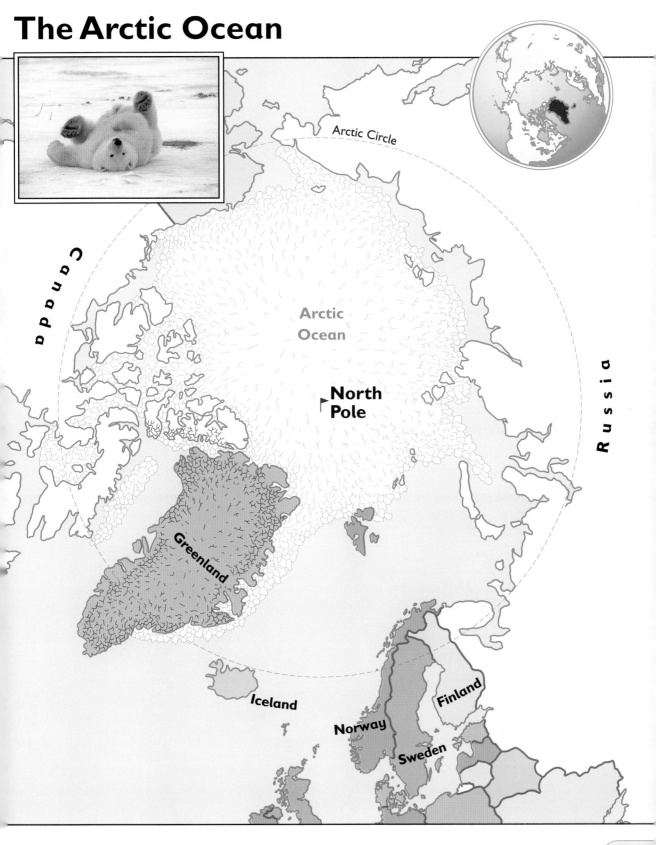

Arctic Circle

Canada

Arctic
Ocean

North
Pole

Russia

Greenland

Iceland

Norway

Finland

Sweden

The Arctic Ocean is frozen water.

World weather

Al Azizyah in Libya

Vostok in Antarctica

The coldest place in the world.

The hottest place in the world.

The Atacama Desert in Chile

Mawsynram in India

The wettest place in the world.

The driest place in the world.

These places have record breaking weather